See for yourself

SCHOOL

Jeff Stanfield

WAYLAND

Homes • School • Shops • The Street • Transport

HOW TO USE THIS BOOK

This book will help you find out about schools. All the questions highlighted in **bold** have answers on pages 26–27, but try to work them out for yourself first. Investigate your own school by trying some of the detective activities on pages 28–29. You'll find difficult words explained on page 30.

Most of the photographs in this book were taken in Cardiff. So you can compare the schools in Cardiff with your own school.

Series editor: Polly Goodman
Book editor: Mike Hirst
Book designer: Jean Wheeler
Cover design: Dome Design

First published in 1997 by Wayland Publishers Ltd
61 Western Road, Hove, East Sussex BN3 1JD, England

© Copyright 1997 Wayland Publishers Ltd

British Library Cataloguing in Publication Data
Stanfield, Jeff
    Schools. – (See For Yourself)
    1. Schools – Wales – Cardiff – Juvenile literature
    2. Schools – Wales – Cardiff – Problems, exercises, etc. – Juvenile literature
    I. Title
    3371'.00942987

ISBN 0 7502 2002 3

Find Wayland on the internet at
http://www.wayland.co.uk

Photographic credits
All the photographs in this book, except those listed below, were taken by Bipinchandra J. Mistry.
Front cover: *lunchbox, ruler, pencil case, calculator and books:* Chapel Studios; *children:* Wayland Picture Library. Pages 4 (top and centre), 8 (top), 11 (top and centre), 12 (bottom), 15 (top), 16 (bottom): Wayland Picture Library.

Typeset by Jean Wheeler, England
Printed and bound in Italy by G. Canale & C.S.p.A., Turin

CONTENTS

GETTING TO SCHOOL

Every morning, thousands of children go to school.

▲ Some walk to school.

◀ Others go by car.

Some children travel to school on ▶ a school bus.

Why do some children go on a bus?

How do you get to your school?

▼ There is a busy road outside this school.

The school crossing patrol stands at the crossing before school starts. He is there after school too.
What does the crossing patrol do?

◀ **What is the picture on the sign?**

How do people cross the road when the crossing patrol is not there?

BRICKS AND STONES

School buildings come in all shapes and sizes.

Look at the two schools on this page.

They are both old. They were built in Victorian times.

◀ This school building used to be a church.

▲ This school is modern. It has only one floor.

Why is it better to have all the classrooms on the ground floor?

◀ The grey buildings are temporary classrooms.
They are quick and easy to build.

They were put up outside the main building when the school needed more space.

When they are no longer needed, they will be taken down.

COME ON IN!

At the start of the day, you see lots of grown-ups outside the school gates.

The school entrance is a busy place at home time too.
It can be dangerous.

▼ **Why should the children in this school be careful at home time?**

◀ Can you see the yellow marks on the road?

They tell drivers not to park outside the school gate.

The metal barrier is for safety. It stops children from running straight out into the road.

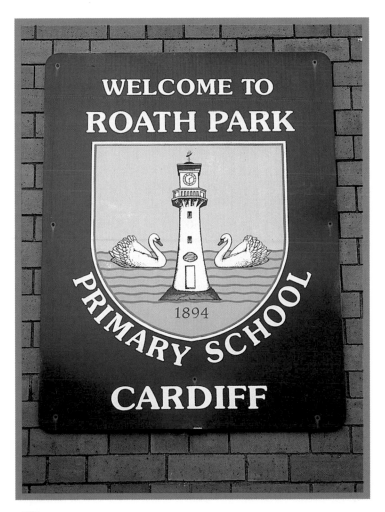

▲ You usually see a name sign at a school entrance.

Find the sign for Roath Park Primary School.

Why does it say '1894'?

GROWN-UPS AT SCHOOL

The grown-ups at school work hard, just like children.

This teacher and classroom ▶ assistant are preparing activities for the children.

They read stories, do playground duty, and mark sums and writing.

How many different things does your teacher do?

◀ The headteacher is the school's leader.

Headteachers sometimes work in their office.

School secretaries are important people.

Like teachers, secretaries do many different jobs.

What is the secretary ▶ **doing here?**

What is the name of your school's secretary?

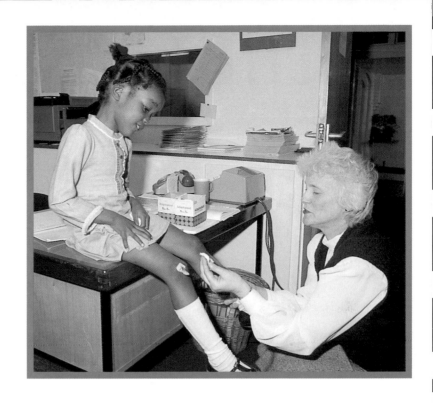

▲ The caretaker looks after the school buildings and equipment.

What is this caretaker doing?

▼ **Who are these people? What job do they do?**

11

IN THE CLASSROOM

You spend most of your time at school in a classroom.
Inside the classroom is the equipment that you need.

◀ **What equipment can you see here?**

Teachers put displays of work on the classroom walls.

◀ **What topic has this class just been working on?**

These girls are putting paper shapes on the window. ▶
Most classrooms have big windows.

Why is it good to have big windows?

12

Classrooms ▶
often have a
space where the
whole class can
sit together on
the floor.

When do you sit
on the floor at
your school?

▼ Look at the furniture in this classroom.
How are the chairs and desk different from
the chairs and table in your home?

**What is special
about the
furniture in
a school
classroom?**

ALONG THE CORRIDOR

The different parts of a school are usually joined by corridors.

You walk along corridors to go from one room to another.

We use corridors in other ways too.

▲ **How is the corridor used in this school?**

◀ You often see coat pegs in the corridor.

Children hang up their coats and bags before they go into the classroom.

Sometimes, children work in the corridor just outside the classroom.

These boys ▶ are using a computer.

Where are computers kept in your school?

◀ These children are busy composing a piece of music.

Why is it a good idea for them to work in the corridor?

15

THE SCHOOL HALL

The hall is usually the biggest room in the school.

▼ This school hall is being used for assembly for the whole school.

◀ This hall also has a stage.

What are school stages used for?

Sometimes school halls are used for lessons.

Look at the equipment ▶ under the window.

Which two lessons take place in this hall?

▲ **What lesson is going on here?**
When the lesson is over, the ropes and climbing bars fold back to the wall.

◄ A group of actors is visiting this school.

They are performing a play in the hall.

How do you use the hall in your school?

A PLACE TO READ

Libraries have a big ▶ collection of books.

There are also desks and chairs for work and quiet reading.

In the library, each book has its own special place.

All the books on one subject are kept together.

◀ **What type of books are on this top shelf?**

Look at the red sign in the shelf to help you.

This library also ▶
has its own
computer.

It has games and
puzzles to help
children learn.

The boy is using
a CD-ROM.

A CD-ROM is a kind of book on a computer.
To work it, you put a disc into the computer.
The pages come up on the screen.
Some pages have moving pictures and sound.

◀ **What does
this display
want pupils
to do?**

PLAYTIME

Playtime is just as important as lesson time.

We all need to have a break between work.

▲ This is a big playground. At playtime, the children go outside for exercise and fresh air.

Is the playground used for anything else?

What game are these ▶ **children playing?**

What is your favourite game at playtime?

The reception class ▶ has its own special part of the playground.

There are tricycles and a slide to play on.

When it rains hard, everyone stays inside. You can do different wet play activities.

◀ These children are playing with the water tub. They really are having a wet playtime!

What do you do at wet playtimes?

AROUND THE SCHOOL

In big cities, some schools have small grounds. There is not much space for grass or trees.

The playground at this ▶ school is quite small. The school buildings are close together.

◀ The children at this school have a beautiful garden outside their front entrance.

What job are they doing?

◄ The school also has a wild area and a pond.

Children often use areas like this in their topic work.

What are the children looking for?

There are many ways of making the playground bright and cheerful.

How has this ► school brightened up an old brick wall?

What are your school grounds like?

SAFE AND SOUND

School must be a safe place for children.
Many schools now have special locks or alarms on the doors.

When visitors come to the school, they ring a bell on the front door.
The school secretary picks ▶ up the intercom to find out who is there.
She presses a button on the intercom to open the gate.

Does your school have an intercom?

◀ This sign is on the school wall.
It gives a message to children.

What is the message?

SAY **NO** TO STRANGERS

SIGN SPONSORED BY ♻ Banc National Westminster

Fire and smoke can kill. Look for fire alarms like this one around your school. ▶

▼ If anyone sees a fire, they must set off the alarm at a red box like this one.

How do you set off the alarm?

This is a fire extinguisher. ▶

What does it do?

ANSWERS TO QUESTIONS

Pages 4–5 Getting to School

Children go to school on a bus if they live too far away to walk.

The crossing patrol stops all the traffic so that people can walk across the road safely. The picture on the sign shows two children walking across a road.

When the crossing patrol is not there, people use the traffic lights to cross safely.

Pages 6–7 Bricks and Stones

If all the classrooms are on the ground floor, the school does not need stairs. Stairs can be dangerous, especially for young children. Stairs are also difficult for any pupils who use a wheelchair.

Pages 8–9 Come On In!

The children at this school should be careful to watch out for traffic because there are lots of cars just outside the school entrance.

The year 1894 is the year that Roath Park Primary School was built. The school is over 100 years old.

Pages 10–11 Grown-ups at School

The secretary is helping a pupil who has hurt her knee.

Dinner ladies cook school dinners and serve them to the pupils.

The caretaker is mending one of the school's chairs.

Pages 12–13 In the Classroom

You can see baskets, books, pens, pencils and paper. Can you also spot the edge of a blackboard?

The class has been learning about food.

Big windows let in a lot of light.

Classroom furniture is quite small, so that it is the right size for the children.

26

Pages 14–15 Along the Corridor

The corridor is used to display children's work. The school also keeps books here.

The children work in the corridor so that their music will not disturb the rest of the class.

Pages 16–17 The School Hall

School stages are used for plays and concerts.

PE and music lessons take place in this hall. There are musical instruments underneath the window.

This is a PE lesson. PE stands for Physical Education.

Pages 18–19 A Place to Read

The red sign shows that there are dictionaries on the top shelf.

The display tells you that reading is fun.

Pages 20–21 Playtime

The playground is used for games lessons. There are markings on the ground for a netball court.

The children are playing hopscotch.

Pages 22–23 Around the School

The children are picking weeds out of the flower bed.

The children are looking for frogs and tadpoles. They are finding out what kind of animals live in the school pond.

Some pupils have painted a cheerful picture on the old brick wall.

Pages 24–25 Safe and Sound

The sign tells children not to speak to people they do not know.

You set off the alarm by pressing it in the middle and breaking the glass.

Fire extinguishers contain a special kind of foam. You spray the foam at a fire to put it out.

DETECTIVE ACTIVITIES

● Find out how the children in your class get to school. Make a tally chart.

● Look at a large-scale map of your home area. Mark the home of each person in your class. Plot out the route they take to come to school. Use a different colour for each person.

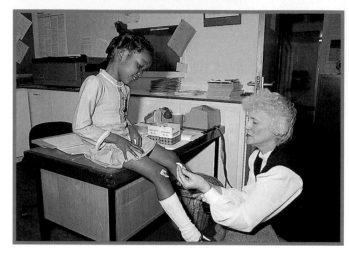

● Find out about the history of your school. (Your headteacher is a good person to ask.) Make a timeline to show the story of your school.

● Make a picture plan of your school building. Label how each area is used.

● Make up signs for the important rooms in your school. Make a sign for the hall, the library, the music area and any other important place. The signs will help new pupils to find their way around your school.

● Make a job-watching trail for your school. The trail must take you to see grown-ups doing as many different jobs as possible.

● Make a display for your classroom to show all the different kinds of work that people do in your school. If you have a camera, you could take photographs of the different kinds of work.

● Make a record of all the places you go to in school in one week. Put your results in a tally chart. Which rooms or areas do you visit most often?

• Make up a question sheet about books. Which is the most popular book in your class? Which book is borrowed most often from the school library?

• Make a plan to improve your playground. What sorts of equipment would you have in it? Would you put markings on the walls or the ground?

• Write out a set of rules for using the playground. The rules should make sure that the playground is a safe and a fair place for each pupil.

• Which is your favourite place in your school? Which place do you like least? Draw a picture of each place and say why you do or do not like it.

• Make your own school-sounds game. Use a cassette recorder to record the sounds in different parts of the school. You can include the creaking of the school gate, singing in assembly and the school bell. Then draw a picture of each place where you made the recording. Play the recordings to your friends. They have to match the sounds with the drawings.

• Make a small sign that means 'Be Careful!' Put the sign at all the dangerous places in your classroom. You should include switches, sharp tools and electric sockets.

• Find out about all the activities that go on in your school hall. Keep a record of how the hall is used each day.

DIFFICULT WORDS

Assembly A time when a lot of people gather together.

Caretaker Someone who looks after a building.

CD-ROM A type of book that comes on a computer disc, with writing, sound and movement.

Composing Making up. A composer is someone who makes up a new piece of music.

Environment The area that we live in.

Equipment The things we need to do a job. To work at school we need equipment such as pens, books and blackboards.

Fire extinguisher A fire extinguisher has a special kind of foam inside. You spray the foam at a fire to put it out.

Grounds The land all around a building.

Intercom A kind of telephone, sometimes called an entryphone. A visitor rings the doorbell and speaks into a microphone next to the bell. Someone inside the building picks up a telephone and speaks to the visitor. Then they press a button to open the door or gate.

Reception class The class that children go to when they begin school.

School crossing patrol Someone who helps people to cross a road at busy times of the day. The crossing patrol has a sign to stop the traffic.

Secretary In school, a secretary works in an office. The secretary's main job is to deal with letters and bills, but she or he often does lots of other jobs besides.

Temporary If something is temporary, it lasts for a short time.

Victorian times A time in history. It lasted from 1837 to 1901, when Queen Victoria was queen. Your great-great-great grandparents were alive in Victorian times.

Wild area A place where grass and trees are allowed to grow wild. Some schools also have a school pond, with water creatures, in their wild areas.

Other Books to Read

History from Objects: At School by Karen Bryant-Mole (Wayland, 1994)

History from Photographs: Schools by Kath Cox & Pat Hughes (Wayland, 1995)

Mapwork 1 by David Flint & Mandy Suhr (Wayland, 1992)

Mapwork 2 by Julie Warne & Mandy Suhr (Wayland, 1992)

Our Schools by Stewart Ross (Wayland, 1992)

School Day by Monica Stoppleman (A & C Black, 1990)

Schools by Ruth Thomson (Watts, 1995)

Schools in Victorian Times by Margaret Stephen (Wayland, 1996)

INDEX

Page numbers in **bold** mean that there is also information about the subject in a photograph.